GRAY WOLF PUP

SMITHSONIAN
WILD HERITAGE COLLECTION

For my children, with deepest love
  — *D. B.*

To Kristin and Lukas
  — *J. D.*

Copyright © 1993 by Trudy Management Corporation,
165 Water Street, Norwalk, CT 06856, and the Smithsonian Institution,
Washington, DC 20560.

Book Design: Shields & Partners

First Edition
10 9 8 7 6 5 4 3 2
Printed in Singapore

Library of Congress Cataloging-in-Publication Data

Boyle, Doe.

Gray wolf pup / by Doe Boyle :
illustrated by Jeff Domm.
          p.   cm.
Summary: Gray Wolf Pup discovers the consequence of disobedience when he
wanders beyond the boundaries of his pack and becomes lost on the tundra.
          ISBN 1-56899-010-3
1. Wolves — Juvenile fiction. [1. Wolves — Fiction.]
I. Domm, Jeff. 1958- ill. II. Title.
          PZ10.3.B715Gr 1993   93-13358
          (E) — dc20   CIP
                                                             AC

GRAY WOLF PUP

by Doe Boyle

Illustrated by Jeff Domm

Soundprints

A Division of Trudy Management Corporation
Norwalk, Connecticut

In the lush plains of Alaska's Central Uplands, Gray Wolf Pup rolls on his back in the warm earth outside the wolf den. With a mischievous look, he scrambles up on his short sturdy legs, nudging his brothers to play with him.

The pups run to the top of a small hill. Their mother and father and the ten other wolves in their pack have made this hill their spring home. Gray Wolf Pup jumps at his littermates from every side and nips at their noses. He is the strongest of the six pups, and he struts around as if he were leader of the pack.

8

But Pup is not the leader of the pack. His father, the alpha male, is in charge. He guides the pack through its territory in the tundra and leads the hunt to find food. The alpha female, Gray Wolf Pup's mother, is there to help him. With the help of the other adult wolves, she feeds the pups and teaches them the pack's rules.

Scampering away from his brothers, Gray Wolf Pup tumbles downhill, landing under the noses of his parents. Nipping their ears and tails, he pesters them until they rise to play with him. When Gray Wolf Pup is too pushy, his father reminds him who is boss, pinning the pup to the ground.

The young wolf licks Father's nose, whining softly.

Tiring of his play, Father sends the lively pup away.
Gray Wolf Pup finds his brothers and leads them toward
the mossy hills of the tundra. He pokes into mouse holes
and prances about with his ears and tail high. Suddenly,
a field mouse darts from behind a boulder. Gray Wolf
Pup forgets that he must not stray too far from home.
He leaves his brothers and chases
the mouse over a ridge.

Gray Wolf Pup races after his prey. He is learning to hunt in the same way he has seen his parents hunt. He pounces at the mouse again and again with his back arched, trying to catch it between his paws.

Soon, however, Gray Wolf Pup is confused. The first mouse has disappeared. Other mice appear and catch Gray Wolf Pup's eye. Excited, Gray Wolf Pup chases after them and is led farther away from home. Before long, all the mice have escaped into their holes. Now Gray Wolf Pup is alone, far out on the tundra. Beyond the safety of the wolf pack and the den, he is not so bold. He is lost and in danger because he is alone. Gray Wolf Pup begins to whimper.

No one hears Gray Wolf Pup's soft cries. His ears droop. His tail drops between his legs. The hills around him all look the same. Gray Wolf Pup does not know how to get home. He begins to howl for his parents. His cries ring out clearly across the stillness.

Back at the wolf den, Mother feeds her pups. She sees that Gray Wolf Pup is missing and she calls to the pup's father. Together they howl into the twilight. They listen. Then, leaving their young in the care of another adult wolf, they head over the ridge to find their lost pup.

Under a clump of willows, Gray Wolf Pup sits, stiff with fear. The wind whistles around him, carrying his voice over the ridges. Soon, his parents appear at the top of the nearest rise. They have followed their pup's scent and sound. He squirms joyfully when he sees them, but he does not run to greet them. He senses he is in trouble.

Father trots toward Gray Wolf Pup with his tail high and his fur fluffed out. His eyes are stern. He crouches low as if to pounce and scolds Gray Wolf with a growl.

Gray Wolf Pup whimpers and rolls on his back. Arching his neck, he reaches up to lick the noses of his parents. He is ready to obey. He will not stray from the pack again. Someday Gray Wolf Pup may be leader of the pack, but not yet. He still has many lessons to learn.

Father leads Gray Wolf Pup and his mother back
to the den. The other wolves run to greet them,
rubbing noses and hugging Gray Wolf Pup's neck
with their paws. The pack is together again.
Every one of the wolves is safe.

From now on, Gray Wolf Pup will follow the pack's rules. He will not wander nor disobey his parents. For now, he will watch and learn and lead his brothers only in play. In time, he may be the alpha male leader.

About the Gray Wolf

The wolf is a wild dog, a member of the family canidae which includes domestic dogs, coyote, jackals and foxes. In appearance, the adult wolf looks similar to a husky or malamute. The wolf pup, however, bears a striking resemblance to German Shepherd puppies.

Wolves travel, hunt and live together in family groups, called the pack. The core of the pack is the alpha male and female — the most dominant members. Their offspring, the pups, constantly test one another to find out who eventually will be "top wolf," the alpha leader. Although they are ferocious predators, wolves are also loyal, affectionate and concerned with the welfare of others within the pack.

Once abundant throughout Europe, Asia and North America, wolves now are endangered in much of their former range. In North America their big footprints can be seen and their choruses of howls can be heard only in remote parts of Alaska, Canada, the Rocky Mountains, northern Minnesota and Isle Royale in Lake Superior.

Glossary

den: a cave, hollow log or hillside burrow where wolf pups are born and raised for the first weeks of their lives.

pack: a group of wolves that live together, sharing the work of hunting and raising young pups.

alpha male: the male wolf, at the top of the pack's social structure, usually dominant as to personality and leadership qualities.

alpha female: the female wolf at the top of the pack's social hierarchy.

tundra: regions with low temperatures and permanently frozen subsoil.

field mouse: a popular name for the meadow vole found in Alaska.

willow: one of the few woody plants that grows on the tundra.

Points of Interest in this Book

pp. 4-31 yellow arctic poppies; mountain avens (white wildflowers); tree-like alder bushes; red-leaved crowberry plants.

p. 12 long-tailed jaeger (bird).

pp. 16, 22 caribou antlers.

p. 18 bald eagle; caribou.